What is the Meaning of Life...
Life Lessons

DEBBIE BRYAN

BALBOA.
PRESS

A DIVISION OF HAY HOUSE

Balboa Press books may be ordered through booksellers or by contacting:

Balboa Press
A Division of Hay House
1663 Liberty Drive
Bloomington, IN 47403
www.balboapress.com
1 (877) 407-4847

Because of the dynamic nature of the Internet, any web addresses or links contained in this book may have changed since publication and may no longer be valid. The views expressed in this work are solely those of the author and do not necessarily reflect the views of the publisher, and the publisher hereby disclaims any responsibility for them.

The author of this book does not dispense medical advice or prescribe the use of any technique as a form of treatment for physical, emotional, or medical problems without the advice of a physician, either directly or indirectly. The intent of the author is only to offer information of a general nature to help you in your quest for emotional and spiritual well-being. In the event you use any of the information in this book for yourself, which is your constitutional right, the author and the publisher assume no responsibility for your actions.

Any people depicted in stock imagery provided by Thinkstock are models, and such images are being used for illustrative purposes only. Certain stock imagery © Thinkstock.

Print information available on the last page.

ISBN: 978-1-5043-4293-3 (sc)
ISBN: 978-1-5043-4294-0 (e)

Library of Congress Control Number: 2015916749

Balboa Press rev. date: 11/10/2015

Dedicated to my family and soul family

In the Beginning

You don't really know what you have and what you don't have when you come to planet Earth. As a child, you think that everyone is exactly the same as you. You don't realize that you are different and not a part of the normal awareness which resides in many sentient beings. You are born aware of your gifts, but without understanding that anything is unusual because they are so natural and free flowing.

As a young child, I would have "dreams" that would always come true later on. I would dream about a happening, but I wouldn't tell my family about it until after the event actually took place. Because I waited until after the fact to tell my parents about my dream, they would just smile, laugh at me and shake their heads as they went along with their day. I never knew I was different from other people by being born with gifts. My parents' non-reactive responses were exactly what I needed to allow me to keep my self-confidence and not turn the dreams and visions away.

Even as a young child, complete strangers would come up to me and tell me that I was so gifted. I had no idea what they meant by this. In fact, these people usually scared me. Between the ages of six and 10, I had no idea what they meant by the word "gifted." One day after Mass, an older lady who was sitting on the complete opposite side of the church, came over to tell me how gifted I was. All I could think of was "Get this crazy lady away from me!" I couldn't believe this type of person was even going to church. Again, I had no idea what having gifts meant, and it wasn't something I heard my parents talk about.

I was four years old when one of the most traumatic events of my life happened. I remember it very well because it was time to go to preschool. This is usually an exciting time in a child's life; a major milestone proving we are growing and maturing. For me, this happy excitement became a cruel reality as I began to realize that not all people are kind and loving! Preschool was a completely foreign environment because this was the first time I experienced children who were unkind to each other. I cried each day my mom dropped me off at school. This was not a place I wanted to be.

Kindergarten was better because I had a really kind teacher, but the cruel reality hit again in first grade when I entered parochial school. I was the girl who was not included in the already formed clique because I had attended a different kindergarten than all the other girls. They excluded me from everything and made fun of me right to my face. I hated being bullied, so I decided I would not be going back to school ever again. I put my plan into action by telling my mom I was sick. But she, like many other moms, said the only way I would be staying home from school was if I had a fever or I was vomiting. So I had to go to school.

Throughout my entire grade school years, I never fit in with most of the girls my age. My experiences with them left me wondering how people, even those who considered themselves friends, could be so horrendously mean to one another and stab each other in the back. I continued to witness these acts throughout my six years of elementary school. I simply could not make sense of this cruel behavior between human beings. I did know this: I could not allow their behavior to change me. I purposed in my heart and soul to be loving and kind no matter what. I chose and set my intention to never be mean, treat anyone badly, and certainly not to ever bully anyone. I had a deep down knowing inside of me that the grade school girls were simply not living God like. No matter how many times I was hurt by their actions, I never changed my loving ways. I knew in my soul that I could never allow myself to become mean like them, and I needed to always treat people better than I would want to be treated.

When I was about eight or nine years old, I always knew when someone in our circle of family or friends was going to die. I really had no idea that other people in the world didn't share in this "knowing." I wasn't sure how I knew, but I never doubted that it was certain to happen. After our loved one would transition from the earth, it was very easy to tell my parents, "I already dreamt that." My fabulous parents would look at me, laugh and say, "Okay." My parents never yelled at me, told me I was lying, or that there is no way I could possibly have known. They simply took my news with a grain of salt and continued on with their tasks at hand. I attribute their reactions to being the helpful force that kept me feeling safe and secure in sharing the knowledge I was given. That comfort took me to a new level of telling my parents who would die next, before it happened. They would listen to me, but this time there were no little laughs. They would not react at all. That made me feel really sad, and I did not want these visions anymore. I began to think I had been cursed. I no longer wanted to know when someone was going to die, let alone who it was. The guilt of not being able to change the outcome was unbearable. It took me some time to realize that my visions were not responsible for the happenings, and that what I was being shown was meant to be. I learned that through receiving these messages, I had the opportunity to say goodbye to my loved ones before they crossed over. That is a true gift!

Why I was able to keep growing my gifts

My parents seemed to have an incredible knack for being great judges of character. I remember hearing my parents' discussions regarding new people they would meet. They would talk with each other about the way the person caused them to feel, and then talk with my siblings and me about it. They described this intuition as having a "gut feeling," and they were always right!

I, too, have always been able to tell if the energy coming from someone I first meet is loving or fear based. Once again, I assumed everyone could feel the "vibes" coming from others, so I wasn't aware that this might be another something special that resided within me. I never once thought it strange to be open to this intuition, or discernment as some may call it. To me it was quite simply "common sense." Remaining open to this intuitive sense is another gift I am forever grateful to my parents for because it has definitely served me as a very valuable tool in my lifetime. They also taught me the value of being open to feelings and following natural instincts while setting aside all bias and judgments.

My dad is one of the most amazing, intelligent and funny men I know. He is amazing because his family is his number one priority! He and my mom had four daughters, and they taught us the importance of family and how to work as a team. My dad made it very clear that there were three very crucial things he expected from each of us: graduate from college, go to church, and vote.

Dinnertime was a very important ritual in our home. It was a time for all of us to connect, reflect on our day together, and especially to laugh. Life without humor is no kind of life at all.

A sweet, funny story I will always remember about my dad, took place at a McDonald's restaurant. Our family was waiting in line behind a grandmother and her grandson. The grandmother was counting her change in order to pay for their meal. My dad, in his quick wit and generosity, handed her a twenty dollar bill and softened the awkwardness by telling her he had won the lottery. My dad never really had much money because he always invested it.

The true lottery he won was the opportunity to be a blessing to this little family. That, my friends, is truly the biggest win we can ever share!

My father can perform any task, except work on cars! He enjoys building things from scratch, learning new technology, and painting beautiful portraits. He is a successful entrepreneur and has been elected to political office. He truly has a zeal and passion for life and learning. Perhaps this is partially linked to the fact that he has been declared clinically dead twice.

The first time was in high school while playing football. He was so forcibly tackled that his spleen ruptured. He was rushed to the hospital emergency room where he was placed in a cleaning room, because all of the treatment rooms were filled with other patients. As my dad tells the story, while in that room, he left his body and saw the hospital staff working to resuscitate his blue, lifeless body. He remembers hearing the doctor saying, "Let's try the paddles one more time." My father came back to life.

When my father was 21 years old, he was sitting with his mother in the hospital. She was losing her fight with breast cancer. My grandmother described to everyone in the room that she saw the most beautiful site she has ever seen. My grandmother was describing Heaven and the overwhelming comfort she felt. When my grandmother crossed over to Heaven she had no fear and was so excited to go to the light of Heaven. At that point my father decided that he would never fear death.

His second close call with death took place when my parents were seven months married and seven months pregnant with me. My parents were boating and waterskiing with friends when my dad suddenly collapsed. They quickly made it back to shore, got my dad into the car, and rushed him to the closest hospital. The doctors told mom that dad had a cerebral aneurysm and would need surgery, but they weren't equipped to perform the surgery he needed. For the next seven days the doctors and nurses were able to get, and keep, dad stabilized until he could be moved. On the seventh day, my uncle, who was the Canton Chief of Police, escorted the transportation of my dad to Mercy Hospital, where he would receive the surgery he needed by neurosurgeon, Dr. Byrd.

Dr. Byrd told my mom that only 1 out of 100,000 patients survive this surgery, and she should prepare herself for what may come. My mom was seven months a bride and seven months pregnant. For seven days she thought she was going to become a widow, a single mother and have to deal with my father's business all alone.

My father clinically died while he was waiting to be treated for his cerebral aneurism. This was the second time he had the opportunity to cross over, but his guides and his mother, who had already crossed over 2 years before the aneurism, knew it wasn't his time. So, he made it through the surgery, and we had another miracle! An absolute miracle! A 1-in-100,000 chance miracle! Dad still has a metal plate in his head, and some loss of taste and smell. I am so grateful that he survived his aneurysm and stayed to be my wonderful father.

After my father clinically died the second time, my parents went back to the Catholic Church. I was raised a very strict Catholic and attended a parochial school from age seven up to seventh grade. My parents always taught us, supported us, and put family first. Still to this day, my mom cooks an incredible Sunday dinner so we can all bond, laugh, and stay close. I am so blessed to have them for my parents. I share these incredible stories with you to show that I was raised by a father who really knew the truth first hand that Heaven is for real.

I feel I was able to keep the gifts I was born with because of the way I was raised. We are all born with the intuitive gifts but our environment seems to numb them. My parents got more involved in the Catholic Church since God gave my father another chance on Earth. I was still raised more spiritual than religious because my parents are very intuitive. Just recently, I was walking into my parents' house, and my mom was listening to her answering machine. The message was from my sister who had just returned to her home after a visit. When she was leaving, my mom said she wasn't going to see my sister's dog again. We all thought the dog was fine and weren't sure what she meant by that statement. The answering machine message from my sister stated mom had been right: the dog wasn't expected to make it through the night. The dog died two days after their return home. When my mom finished listening to the message, she looked at me and said, "You got that from me!" I had to laugh when I heard her taking credit for the "sense of knowing." It was very important that my parents were supported in their own gifts so they could allow me to keep mine. I am so blessed I didn't have to shut my gifts down like most children do when they arrive on Earth.

Often our environment and man-made teachings passed down from generation to generation block the spiritual gifts we all have had since birth. One of those gifts is intuition, the sense of knowing something without being able to explain it. The key to unlocking this, and other gifts, is connecting with Source through meditation.

Meditation calms the mind and stops the chatter in your head. Usually when we slow down, we start to think what we need to do next, or what we forgot to do. Some even start to worry about things. But that is what I call, "mind chatter." Meditation is complete silence of the mind. I suggest that you sit up with your feet flat on the floor, not crossed. Always say, or set, your intention by asking for Source's highest connection, light, and protection. Rest your arms beside you, then start at your feet and relax every muscle in both feet. Move up your calves and relax every muscle, then move up to you thighs and relax those muscles. Move up to you head and release all the tension. Now you feel like you can just melt into the chair. Next, take a color that pops into your head, or one you see if you close your eyes. Take that color and start at your feet wrapping that color for protection around your feet, your legs, your torso, up and over the head. Finish by make a bow with the color since you are a gift from God.

Now your mind is silent. Take deep breaths; breathe in love and exhale stress. With each breath, you go deeper into your subconscious. You are not in control but you are safe, loved, and protected. I like to meditate with my eyes closed so I know the message is the truth and my ego doesn't get in the way. So close your eyes and watch between your eyes. That's where the third eye is located. Watch it like an intense movie. You should start seeing some grey over the black. Keep watching, and you may see pictures. Others will have the sense of "knowing." Whatever you see or know when your mind is clam, the message you receive is truth. The biggest hurdle is to trust what you see or feel. Start with 10 minutes every day and work on meditating. It's the key to connecting with Source.

The Other Side

When I became an adult, I was living my life like a crazy woman: nonstop coming and going. One summer, I had been swimming every day, multiple times a day, only wearing sandals and not paying attention to my body. The skin on my foot must have dried out, but I didn't notice until it cracked open. It really hurt, but rather than slow down and see a doctor, I decided to medicate it with Neosporin. It was a great idea! I put on the Neosporin and wrapped my foot with gauze. I went to bed thinking I'd wake up in the morning and it would be better. I slept well throughout the night, as I recall, but I awoke in the morning with a blister the size of a softball that went from my heel up to my ankle. I was shocked! What in the world happened?

I got up and began to get ready for my workday in spite of it. As I was getting ready, I felt pain because the blister was so huge and tight. But, still not wanting to slow down, I decided to poke it. It took forever to drain! I tidied it all up and went to work. Later that day I had a doctor friend look at it. He said I was having an allergic reaction to the Neosporin, and I would have to rest for the next couple of days. The entire affected area of skin on the inside of my heel and ankle all peeled back so there was nothing but raw flesh showing. It was so painful!

My doctor ordered me to rest with my foot elevated 24/7. I continued to go to work anyway and simply elevated my foot on a pillow I would place on a chair. When I got home, I would elevate my foot above my heart on a couch in my bedroom. My father told me in a no nonsense tone that if I didn't take care of my foot properly I could lose it. That definitely put things in perspective for me because I certainly didn't want to lose my foot!

It was very difficult for me to just sit and keep my foot elevated. I desperately wanted to be out in the sun, but all I could do was wait for my foot to heal. There was, however, a master plan for being off of my foot; it gave me endless hours to meditate.

During the first couple of days while I was meditating on the couch, Archangel Uriel came into my room with a puzzle. I was sitting with my foot elevated, so I know I wasn't sleeping. I watched Uriel as he put the first part of the puzzle together. It said, "What is the Meaning of Life..." And then he put the rest of the pieces together and they spelled out, "Life Lessons." Then Archangel Uriel said to me, "I will show you over the next few weeks exactly what I mean." After he completed the puzzle, he left. I began to contemplate what he had shown me. I felt that a part of me already knew this concept, and he was just reawakening my soul.

Uriel came back the next day and told me he was now going to show me what he meant about yesterday's puzzle. He actually took me to the other side. The first thing he showed me was a teenage girl driving her car, and then a man driving his car. I watched this happening like watching a movie. The man drove through a red light and crashed straight into the young girl's car; the door on the driver's side. The collision killed her on impact. The young girl was so beautiful and seemed to have an amazing life ahead of her. It was very sad to see this happening right before my eyes. I watched as the policemen arrived and discussed how the man who hit the car was drunk and hadn't stopped for the light. The drunken driver didn't have any life threatening injuries.

Uriel then took me to the heavenly realm and showed me how this event ruined the lives of two families. The young girl's family was so devastated over the loss of their beautiful daughter that they clung to resentment and anger until they were so bitter that they wanted the drunk driver dead. They fully and angrily believed that this man had stolen their daughter's life. The parents never chose to truly recover from the loss of their daughter, and the resentment they held onto against the drunken driver broke their own family apart. Anger and resentment destroyed the young girl's family. Although the parents still had two living children at home, they never looked at them the same way they did before the accident. Their focus was instead on hate and vengeance. The young girl's parents had so much hate and resentment that it tore their marriage apart. Their children, feeling and experiencing all of the negativity from their parents, ended up rebelling and having problems. The young girl's parents divorced, and the entire dynamics of their family unraveled in tumultuous ways.

Uriel showed me the drunken driver's life. He had been the sole provider for his family, while his wife stayed home and cared for their children. When he went to jail, his wife was forced to find a job. Unfortunately, no one would hire her because of the fatal accident her husband had caused. She lost the house and ended up on the street, while the children were taken away and placed in foster care. Not one person could be found who cared to help them. She and the children were penalized by the judgment of others for the actions of her husband. The driver's wife became very bitter, divorced her husband, and vowed to never go visit him in jail. The children disowned their father and carried the burden of the event their entire lives. I just could not get over how the incident instantly changed the dynamics of both families in such a detrimental way.

The reason why I got to see what happened to both families was to show me life is really about learning lessons. I can honestly say that when Uriel told me that the meaning of life was "life lessons," a light bulb went off in my head, and my soul remembered why I was here. My soul and heart knew we are usually with our soul family. A contract is created by individual souls and their guardian angels. It is written with the assistance of our soul families before we are born to help our souls evolve. Then Uriel showed me that the girl and the drunk driver were part of a soul family. Prior to this lifetime they had loved each other very, very much. The tie between the driver and the young girl was so close.

Uriel then said to me, "Let me show you what this is all about. This is about the life lessons that you contract before you even come down to Earth." Uriel reminded me that there are no coincidences in life. Our angels are always working to keep our contracts intact. He then took me to a circular room 10 feet in diameter. I call this the viewing room. He said this is where we watch our lives from birth to crossing over. Uriel told me we are our own critics. God does not judge. We are the only ones who get to judge the actions during our lives; how we interacted and reacted in every moment. The reason why we come down to Earth is to grow our souls to be God like. And God is unconditional love. There is no judgment or fear from God.

Uriel showed me that the drunk driver and the young girl had a contract before they came down to Earth. Our souls have many lives. During one of those lifetimes, we must experience the tragic death of a loved one. Their contract for this tragic accident was made to give everyone involved, especially their families, the opportunity to learn life lessons regarding forgiveness, compassion, and unconditional love. Sadly, they did not learn these lessons. These families will need to return to Earth again to learn these lessons in another life or their souls will not grow. But we can learn from this example. We can apply the message to other situations that cross our paths.

A few days later, I received a visit from Archangels Uriel, Gabriel, Michael and Rafael. They came in as I was lying down with my foot up. They announced that they were taking me to the place we call Heaven. There are different spheres in Heaven, and I got to go all the way up to the highest realm, which is the God realm. Here in the God realm, I watched what happens when a person crosses over and chooses to come to the light.

Although Heaven's light is always on and does not flicker like other lights, the portal to Heaven is not always open. The soul usually stays on

Earth up to 72 hours after a funeral or wake to console loved ones. Then the portal to Heaven opens and ready souls cross to Heaven.

Once souls reach the light, they are met by their guardian angels. Their guardian angels then take them into the light. This light is always a bright, shining beacon full of everything beautiful and peaceful. There is so much love in this light that it is impossible to walk away from it. Upon reaching Heaven, souls are met by all of their loved ones and pets that have crossed over before them. Their previously deceased loved ones welcome them, and they can spend any amount of time together they desire, since there is no time in Heaven. Yes, time is endless here.

God is in the highest realm. The highest vibration is the 13th vibration. This is a male-female energy that is the most loving, amazing energy you could ever want to be around. God is not labeled as God. There are no labels here. We, for our own intellectual purposes, have labeled God to be many things. We have initiated religious movements and dogmas, rules and laws to support our beliefs. However, the truth is that all religions have the same source. What you choose to label that energy is no more significant than what another labels it.

What is significant is that God is pure unconditional love, the most beautiful feeling you could ever want to experience. I am so blessed to have been able to go there and experience true unconditional love with my own eyes and emotions. I now understand why we want to be God like energy.

I was taught that there is only one rule on the other side: Treat everyone better than you want to be treated. If you can do that with every breath you take, then you are living God like. This is the golden rule we are called to live every moment and with every breath.

Pour out unconditional love that always sees, speaks, and believes the very best is possible for every single being on Earth. God is always unconditional love. God always treats all people better than they want to be treated. That is how we are supposed to act in this lifetime in every situation, because when we leave Earth and enter Heaven, our guardian angels take us to the viewing room. It is here that we watch our lives and see where we missed opportunities to give unconditional love, and where we were spot on. We judge our own lives as we view them on the movie-like screen. Our guardian angels are always beside us for assistance as we review all of the encounters and opportunities given to us to treat others better than we would want to be treated ourselves. Although we may miss opportunities to evolve our souls, we may choose to come back to Earth to work on those lessons. As long as we learn these lessons in the long run, we are growing. From this day forth, remember that in every situation we encounter, we are being given the opportunity to be God like.

When my foot was in the air and my head was in the clouds, I was also shown how every soul begins on sphere one. We come down to the hardest realm of Earth because Earth is the only realm with free will and ego. Many of the souls' lifetimes have been stuck on sphere one because they haven't understood why they were here. It seems inherently natural to want to blame everyone for our problems and become the "poor me," or "oh, woe is me" victim, rather than taking ownership of our actions. We can easily get in the mindset of always thinking of our own selves and how we can get ahead. We are even willing to hurt other people in the process just to have our own way. If we leave Earth with this same consciousness, our soul hasn't evolved and we become stuck on that sphere of Heaven. But, eventually we will grow and advance to the next sphere. Most people on Earth are between the third and eighth sphere of Heaven.

Let me introduce you to Earth Angels. Earth Angels are beautiful souls who have chosen to return to Earth to help people remember why they are here. Earth Angels have already earned their wings in Heaven. Earth Angels don't have to come back to the earthly realm. They can stay in the heavenly realm and work as angels. But some choose to come back to Earth, hence the name Earth Angels. They also help the planet evolve by raising Earth's vibrations. These beautiful angels signed up to come back to Earth. They did not have to come back. I'm sure many of you have had contact with Earth Angels. Earth Angels usually come into your life to help with a problem then, once you turn your head, they are gone without a trace. You just scratch your head and ask, "Where did that person just go"?

Earth-bound Souls

Many souls who suffer traumatic deaths are usually very confused and don't go to the light. They do not acknowledge they have died, and their souls become earth bound. They get very frustrated because their living loved ones can't see them. These souls can cause a lot of heartache and chaos. They can only go to the light of Heaven with the guidance of someone, such as an Earth Angel who is blessed to know how to open the portal of Heaven's light for them. This earthly guide will open the portal and direct them to the light. There is another option. A loved one who is already in Heaven and has become angelic can intervene to assist earth-bound souls go to the light.

Two Surprise Visitors

I was visiting a friend when Mother Mary and Mary Magdalene came to me. They showed me a heart with an infinity sign towards the bottom of the heart. I thought this symbol was beautiful. Both Marys told me that it means unconditional, endless love; the key to Heaven. I tried for almost three weeks to see who was using this sign. I couldn't find it associated with anything except jewelry and tattoos. The two Marys returned and told me the symbol was for me. I trademarked it for my website, yourspiritalhealer.com or angeldebbie.com. I had it made into a sterling silver pendant to wear on a chain around my neck. When I am wearing it, people always stop and tell me how beautiful it is.

Miracles Firsthand

When my son was six years old, we were at the swim club my parents owned. My son heard sirens and rushed to look at the commotion outside the chain linked fence area. There had been a car wreck on the street. He watched in amazement as the responders cleared the damage, and the ambulance took the injured passengers away.

Then he started to run to the pool area and ran across the tennis court, at full steam. He forgot about the tennis net! He ran directly into the net, and it "clothes lined" him! He came to me, crying. When I looked at his head, it looked like he had two scratches on the top of his head. My son was always over active and getting hurt. Although his eyes were dilating, he still had his ornery wits about him. We packed up and drove home. Before I could get the car unpacked, he started vomiting fresh blood. I rushed him to the hospital.

The ER doctor said he had a multiple skull fracture. My son was hit so hard that his head ricocheted and cracked the other side of his skull. My son was life-flighted to a children's hospital because this hospital did not have a pediatric neurosurgeon on its staff. I began to pray. I saw very large male hands. I looked up and said, "You aren't taking him from me." But I was very calm. I didn't understand what the hands meant at that time. My son was prepped for surgery. They needed to wait through the night because he was bleeding so profusely and his brain was very swollen.

My parents brought my daughters to see their brother. My father later told me he thought this would be the last time he would ever see my son alive. It was around midnight when he was driving the girls back to my parents' house. My father was too upset to pay attention to his gas gauge, and he ran out of gas on the highway. He started walking to the next exit to get gas. Out of nowhere appeared an old, beat up station wagon driven by an old man wearing very tattered clothes. The man asked my dad if he needed a ride. The man said he was a trucker and drove my father to get gas. My dad told him about his grandson's critical condition. The man said he would pray for him. He drove my dad back to the car as quickly as possible. When they returned with the gas, my dad went to thank the man, but the man and his car had vanished. He never saw the man again. Yes, there was angelic help involved here, and there was even more to come.

At the hospital, I started to barter with my guides. I told my guides that they could take my life and save my son's since he was so young and had so much to live for. There was much bartering and praying. I was the only one with him. It was the middle of the night with no one around except the nurse at the nurse's station.

My son was put on a prayer line earlier that night, and I could feel all the prayers and love friends, family and even strangers were sending us. Then about 3:00 a.m., I just put my hands on my son's upper chest. I gave all the love from my heart. I wanted to take away his pain. I envisioned him healed. I saw his chest and head being covered in an amber swaying energy. I couldn't stop crying. The feeling was like no other I had ever felt. I cried until my shirt was soaking wet. There was still no one around. My son was sleeping, but heavily medicated.

The next morning the neurosurgeon came with the results from my son's latest CT scan. He said, "This is why I love my job. Your son had a miracle and his head healed without surgery." The neurosurgeon said my son would have loss of motor skills and maybe lose one of his senses because he had a severe head trauma. After all the testing and home visits by a study group, no one could see any damage from the trauma. My son even graduated one of the top of a very large graduating class. He is now studying to be a doctor. I also know now that the large hands meant he was in God's good hands.

Several years after the injury, I ran into the medium who I had worked with before my son's head injury. She just came over and had to tell me that yes, I saw a miracle. She couldn't tell me what, or why, she was told that. She told me that I was very blessed to be a part of a miracle. And right then and there I again thanked Source for the beautiful gift that was bestowed on my son.

Connected

I was sitting at a traffic light on a busy four-lane road when I saw a father and son walking on the side of the road. The son looked to be around five years old. He was walking next to the traffic, between the traffic and his father. In my mind I said to myself, "Really dad! You can't let your son walk on that side!" I was quite disgusted with the father. My windows were up, so he couldn't hear me if I had yelled at him. But as soon I finished my thought I saw the father yank his son away from the traffic and switch sides with him. His son was now shielded from the busy traffic by his father. Then Source told me that I made that happen. And right then and there I realized how powerful our thoughts are and how we are connected in this divine matrix of life.

I teach a class at a holistic center. I told the class about how my thoughts made the father change sides with his son to protect him from the traffic. While I was describing what happened, there were quite a few people who reported getting chill bumps when I told them that my thought made the father protect his son. Chill bumps are confirmation that you are hearing or seeing the truth. I thanked those who shared feeling chill bumps.

After class a few of us wanted to grab a bite to eat. I was driving in the lead with two cars behind me as we drove to the restaurant.

Low and behold I saw a mother and daughter walking down the side of another busy street. The daughter was on the street side, between the traffic and her mother. They were about half of a block ahead of us. I started yelling in my head that the mother needs to switch sides and protect her daughter. I knew that both cars behind me could see them walking, and I kept yelling in my head for them to swap sides. All I could think was that I was failing my test since I just talked about it in class, and I couldn't get the mother to change sides. I kept saying in my head, "Really Mom! You need to protect your daughter!" And the mom still didn't swap sides. As soon as my car was almost beside them, the mom yanked her daughter to the inside, away from the traffic. The mom gave me a very mean look, but I was cheering in my car. As soon as we came to a red light, I got out of my car and turned to face my friends to see if they had seen what had just happened. They both witnessed it and confirmed that our thoughts are indeed powerful. We need to keep our thoughts and words positive because we are all connected to each other in this divine matrix.

Three Channelings for Debbie

Channeling occurs when someone enters a meditative trance, taps into the Source and delivers messages to others in attendance. I attended three sessions and here are the messages I received.

First Channeling - *May 19, 2013*

My daughter you sparkle. Not all people sparkle as you do, and you are multicolor.

It is because there are so many avenues The Holy enters you. Does this make sense to you?

There are different energies entering you, intensities. I would think this would be quite disorienting. You have learned to filter them. You have learned to focus. My daughter you were gifted before you were born. Does this make sense to you? You had a purpose, and when you came into this existence you my daughter, you came with a great deal of certainty. Does this make sense to you? No one could ever tell you about God. Nobody could teach you about God. The stories, yes, they were engaging because they told so much more. Yes, but you felt the certainty. You had the knowing. You had the knowing. You know the source of this knowledge. It comes from the beyond. You did not totally forget. No! You came into this existence with a memory. It's not so much a memory. It's a sensation.

You know the gathering. Does this make sense to you? You know the feel of the gathering. You know the wisdom of the gathering. You know the companionship of the gathering. You know the healing power of the gathering. So my daughter, you have spent your time seeking the gathering, and you have not been satisfied. May I tell you something? Every gathering you find will only be a shadow of the one you know because you know the sacred gathering. You can nurture, and you can guide. Does this make sense to you?

My daughter you have a gift for hospitality, but you resist it, but it brings you satisfaction. You resist it because this was a role imposed upon you. But when you chose it on yourself, there were blessings. Does this make sense?

It has been turmoil. My daughter you have been spun, and you have been thrown down, but never have you lost your knowing. You knew it could never be taken away. So I see The Holy coming into your ears. I see that you see; you have the spiritual sight. My daughter your hands sparkle. There is warmth in your hands. Your heart glows, and it is a mark of compassion.

Your throat is also tight. You are a messenger. My daughter, I would think the number of voices you hear would be quite confusing. Does this make sense to you? There is a unity of the multiplicity in the nature of The Holy; the unity of the multiplicity. I tell you in The Holy we are indeed like we are stars. We are constellations or groupings. Certainly we are all connected. But there is intimacy in the gathering. For my daughter the gathering that surrounds you. It is your family that surrounds you. Does this make sense to you?

My daughter, you feel the emotions that are all around you. You are a bit of a sponge: you take it on, but you have learned to ring it out; to purify. It has made it difficult to be in crowds I would think. So much to read. So much to filter.

My daughter, you're a quick judge of character as well. It is a guttural feeling to you. Does this make sense to you? I can see it. It was discernment. Your mind is inspired. You have learned to use this as a gift. You see the part and the whole. Not all can see this. You see the part and the whole as they are related. Does this make sense to you? You have sight and orientation.

Second Channeling –
August 11, 2013

I see the glow that is your spirit. I see the light that is your soul. It is an honor to be among you.

I shall speak to you of burden. I shall speak to you of labor. For my daughter you are injured by your burden. It is time for the labor to be complete. How can your labor deliver you from your burden? This is the great question for the season of your life. How can your labor deliver you from your burden?

My daughter, it is not for you. The gifts that come are not for you. The children you bear are not for you. The identity you have is an illusion. So why do you cling? I shall speak straight to you today, for you are in the time of great transition. You are at a time of revelation. The revelation is upon you, the epiphany has come. And now there's choice. You are burdened my daughter. Do you know what I mean? There are so many things that burden you. You are responsible for so much. Do you feel it? My daughter it is not your burden. You are not responsible for all of this my daughter. My daughter you are in labor. Do you understand this? There is so much coming through you. There is so much to be given and delivered. My daughter, when does the deliverer find deliverance? You're in labor my daughter. The Holy is coming through you. You understand this to be so. The Holy is coming through you. How shall you deliver what The Holy demands? This also is a burden. Why would The Holy burden you? I'm not only playing with words my daughter, I'm speaking straight, for you are gifted to be the deliverer.

My daughter you are entitled to deliverance. You are burdened, but you are entitled to freedom. It is not for you, and it is not yours.

Step out my daughter. I see you confined. Who encased you? You can break out, my daughter, of the shell. You can crack it. You can break out. The child you gave birth to is yourself. It is your soul. It is your purpose. God among us. God among us!

How do you let go of yourself, my daughter? And how do you realize that God is always with you? My daughter this boy that becomes a man; do you know it is mysterious that you have cast away your own masculinity? Does this make sense to you? You have been placed in this shell. You have not created it, but you are in it. You have sought to grow beyond it, and now it is time to break out. It is time to be delivered.

My daughter, your vision is true on so many levels I can't explain it to you. On every sphere it is true, and you understand the spheres. It is not just time. Some would call it dimension. On every sphere it is true, the birthing my daughter. It is also true for you. My daughter you give birth every moment of your living. You receive, and you deliver. You are a messenger. Do you know what this means? You are a deliverer. You are an organizer. You are a spokesperson. You are a receiver my daughter. It is overwhelming to receive so much, to be burdened to deliver so much.

Let go my daughter. It is not to be a burden. It is to be a fulfillment. Everything you hold dear to you will remain. Everything you protect is protected. Everything you plant shall grow with or without you, for the growth does not come from you, and the protection does not come from you, and the labor does not come from you. It comes through you. So be a conduit my daughter and not a sponge. You have become a sponge, and it is time to ring it out.

Your joints, my daughter cry out to you for there is inflammation. Let go my daughter. Let go. You are filled with The Holy. The Holy soaks into you, and the world needs a balm. You are the gift. You are the gift, and you are the messenger. It is not a burden but a fulfillment. Do you see my daughter? God indeed is with us. A child is born. A growth takes place.

The surrender must be completed. You must surrender to receive. You must empty in order to be filled. You must collapse in order to be raised up. Are you tired my daughter? Then stop. Rest. I do not say abandon all that you have held so dear. I simple say it's not for you that comes through you. It will continue to come through you whether you like it or not. You know this to be true. You cannot shut it down. You don't need to shut it down. The Holy will flow. The Holy will flow. The water will come through you. Let it flow. It is not to be controlled. It is to be accepted. Does this make sense to you? It is to be accepted.

It is a blessing to see you, to recognize you and name you. I shall tell you something more. I recognize you. I have seen you on many spheres. You have a slippery soul. You have slipped out of yourself. It is confusing my daughter to be a journeyer, for the other spheres do not abide by the same laws as we say. It is another reason why you have confined yourself into this shell. You understand the shell even as you hate the shell.

Be free. Be free. Be delivered. You have been in labor long enough, and the burden is great. It is time my daughter. The revelation is at hand. The epiphany has come. Your shell is cracked, and your soul peaks forth. Peak-a-boo. I see you. Come out. Come out where ever you are. Shall The Holy pick away the shell? There is light up

here where I am. Follow the voice to The
Holy. Come out. Come out.

Third Channeling –*October 13, 2013*

*My daughter Debbie, I see you and the you
that is in you. The challenge is to release
the you within you. You know it is there. You
see it and it makes sense to you. The Holy
flows through you: confuses you, confounds
you, inspires you and guides you.*

*You have so many openings it is difficult
to monitor. How do you shut one window
and the other one opens; then you realize
there are too many windows open. You're
not even aware of them. And there are
walls within walls within you. How many
structures are there? Are you a mansion?
Are you doorway, or are you a gateway?*

My daughter, you are full of holes. These holes are not a defect. The holes are an opportunity. There are so many ways you can be filled with The Holy. There are so many ways to decipher and filter. Is this not so? It is a wonderful thing. You are gifted to have such openings to The Holy. With such gifts come liabilities.

You must discover the you that is within you. This is counter to the guidance you usually receive. Usually you are to receive the you within you, and this is true in you. But you also need to discover the you. It is right there. Many people discover by releasing. You must discover by seeking. My daughter you have released so much. You are so beyond yourself. You have received so much.

How then do you define your role of your soul? The role of your soul. It is a difficult balance for there is a purpose in you and for

61

you. It is not an identity but a purpose. Most people define their purpose by expanding. You have expanded so far. My advice to you is to gather yourself. Rediscover the you that's within you, and you will discover that you must lock off some openings. Just for a moment. Just for a time. Just for a season. Does this make sense to you?

Come into your garden and sit with yourself. Speak only what you discover yourself. See only what you garden reveals to you. Come into your garden, and you will find everything you have seen, heard or felt is right here, but in a way you can understand, decipher, and accept. You will also discover you are not alone in your garden. There are benches in your garden, and many people who are willing to sit with you.

There is imbalance around you. Too many demands. Too many opportunities. You are spinning. The manifestations within your body are reflections. They are metaphors. So this time I shall tell you to release. Release everything that is not you. Surrender everything that is not you. Reject everything that is not you. And you will discover the you that is within you. And once you've discovered this, you will realize this is a blessing to be given. Does this make sense to you?

I see you. I see the core within you. I tell you that you are blessed and gifted. You are to be shared. My daughter, collect the kindling within your garden, and light the fire pit within your garden. Let your embers of your soul ignite, and you will find it to be warm and comforting and soothing because the fire is you, and the fire is The Holy, and you my daughter are ready to be ignited. So bring kindling to your fire.

So what is the kindling? Expectations and demands, the confusions and the pains.

Burn them all! And then you shall find the essential you. It is an invitation to the beyond. Go within your garden. It is not time to add. It is time to decrease. It is not time to take in; it is time to limit. Do not add more vitamins or minerals. Trim down to the essentials. Then you will find balance. It is time for a great give away. Not of what you possess, but of what you think. When you give all away, you will find people will bring you the essentials; then you find balance. It is a difficult path my daughter. There's no doubt about it. It will take great discipline. But the blessings are before you and you can see them. You are The Holy.

Readings

Ann

Ann was a friend who scheduled an urgent reading. I had met with her for readings before, and her dad was always ready to come in. She never doubted my gifts. When we met, I told her an old-school baseball player came in, and his image was in black and white. She had no idea who was with us. Eventually he told me his name was Lou Gehrig, and he was working with Ann to amend her contract. Ann gasped, and I continued channeling Lou.

This is the message I channeled from Lou to Ann, "You asked for an early exit from Earth. I heard you and allowed you to change your contract." Ann told me she had been diagnosed with ALS, Lou Gehrig's disease, the day before. She knew she needed to see me as soon as possible.

Lou showed me the scene where Ann was talking with her angels and saying she wanted to be finished with her life's lessons. She asked for an exit strategy to reach Heaven, and said she didn't want to return to Earth ever again. Ann told me that was exactly the conversation she had with her angels several months ago. She said she remembered the exact day she had this conversation with them.

I began to cry, but my tears were from joy. I saw that Ann's prayers were answered. Ann was so blessed to be able to have completed her growth. The vision I saw showed that it was Ann's time to cross over to Heaven. I saw that Ann would become an angel as soon as she entered Heaven without first going to the viewing room to evaluate her life. I had never seen anyone bypass the viewing room!

I told Ann that I was here for her with anything she needed. Her body quickly deteriorated, and within a few months Ann was in hospice care. Ann summoned me to her bedside several times and asked me to tell her again what I saw for her when she crossed. She told me that she was not able to see it and needed to hear this comforting reassurance.

Ann's time on Earth was getting shorter. A friend texted me and asked if I could come to the hospice center. Ann could barely speak, but I knew what she said. Ann told me that I had a message for her, and I said, "I do?" Then I asked my guides. This was the message I had for Ann, "Look for me, and I will help you cross over." This was the first time I had been told anything like this.

Several days later around 10:30 p.m. when I began to meditate, I saw Ann. She was stuck in the hospice center. When I reached out my hand, Ann took my hand and crossed to the light of Heaven. I saw that she did not go to the viewing room. Ann was met by her loved ones and guardian angels. As soon as she crossed over, she immediately became an angel. Ann had earned her wings. I had never seen this happen before. What an amazing site to watch! Ann immediately started to work. She visited all of her loved ones on Earth to help them begin to heal. Ann was so happy and had such a wonderful disposition. She kept telling me that I was right. Heaven is for real!

Lynn

Lynn came for a session, and it was the first time I met her. We introduced ourselves, and I explained how a session usually goes. I let the angels talk first, and then it goes to your questions. Hopefully when the angels are finished speaking, all of your questions will already have been answered. Lynn said she wasn't sure she had too many question, but she was willing to just listen.

The very first thing I saw was a soccer field. I saw little guy about seven years old running around the soccer field playing the game of soccer. I thought one of the little players was her son, and I asked if her son played soccer around the age of seven. Lynn said yes, he did. I told her I saw the boys in green and gold uniforms. Lynn confirmed those were the colors of her son's team uniforms.

I was watching the scene where I saw her little boy go over to the side of the field. He was playing in the game. Nobody was around while he was going for the ball towards the sidelines. I saw an angel come down and talk to him. The angel asked if he was willing to take on this lesson for his family. He agreed to take on this task. Then I saw him fall on the soccer field. Nobody was around him to push, or trip him. He was all alone. In the next vision I watched, this little guy could not get up. He was paralyzed. I kept watching the vision over and over again, trying to understand where the trauma was. I kept asking to be shown what caused the accident.

I told Lynn that I couldn't see an accident that happened to paralyze her son. I told her exactly what I saw. Lynn explained that there was no accident. There was no trauma to her son on the soccer field. It happened exactly the way I saw it. Lynn explained that her son was on the field and fell over. When they got to him, he was paralyzed from his waist down. I was speechless since I got to see why her son was paralyzed. I told Lynn about how the angel came in and her son agreed to take on the trauma to teach his family about unconditional love and many other lessons. He loved his family so much that he was going to take on this life changing event.

Lynn told me that her son was now 15 years old. For eight years they had traveled all around the United States taking him to many doctors and having many tests performed. Each time they got the same results. No one could tell them why their son was paralyzed from his waist down.

It was a very exhausting and stressful time for them. They spent so much money and resources to keep hitting a dead-end. All they wanted to do was to see how they could help him. But no one could tell them why this had happened. So before Lynn made the appointment with me, she made the decision to accept what happened without any questions; they would never know how he became paralyzed. Lynn and her family came to the realization that they couldn't change what happened, and they weren't going to figure out why it happened.

When they finally were at peace with the incident, Lynn met me for a session. Lynn was amazing. After hearing the story explaining what had happened, she laughed and told me that timing is everything. It had taken her eight years to accept the situation. Once she did, her guides gave her the answers she was seeking. I applauded her for her outlook.

We talked about learning life lessons being the goal of why we are here. I did get to share another vision with her. I saw her son walking with some device that went under his arms like crutches that could help him walk. That vision made her smile from ear to ear. She told me that that was probably the only question she really had, and the angels answered it for her.

Mark

I met Mark for the first reading. He was very apprehensive about the reading and wrote down every word. He was really sure that he was supposed to ask questions, but I let the angels talk. They told Mark that he wasn't happy at all in his marriage, his wife was manipulating him, and they were not on the same spiritual journey. I talked about many events that had happened in the marriage, that Mark was far more spiritually evolved than his wife, and that she would never catch up.

Mark just took notes, but later he told me that he thought he was very happy being married. He said I described his wife perfectly, and there was no way I could have known some things that happened in his marriage because his family didn't even know.

The angels told him that he would leave his marriage and would meet someone at work.

The woman at work would be a perfect spiritual match for him, and they would grow together in synchronicity. He thought I was way off on the whole marriage issue and finding true love at work. There was no one at work he would ever consider dating if he were single.

Mark began to meditate and started doing deep, inner work. He and his wife went to marriage counseling for over a year. When the marriage fell apart, Mark decided to move out. After he found another place to live, he magically found himself attracted to a woman at work. He had a huge crush on her. He couldn't explain how and why it happened. Mark would call me and ask how he should approach her to start a conversation. Mark didn't think he had a chance with her because Mark's best friend at work was talking to her. Mark thought she was attracted to him.

I kept telling Mark that she was the woman I saw and that she would give him a chance.

He got the nerve to talk to her, and they have been inseparable ever since. I've become good friends with both of them, and it was so sweet to hear how much alike they are. Neither one had any idea they had so much in common and were on the same spiritual path. They continue to grow spiritually together. It's so amazing to watch their relationship get stronger.

Jim

My phone was ringing and displaying "blocked call." I let those calls go to voicemail. When I got three more calls in a row from the blocked caller, I decided to answer it because the caller wouldn't leave a message. Luckily I could get to the phone. This man wouldn't give me his name or number.

He told tell me that he didn't believe in Heaven and angels and that he wanted to prove I was a fake. He asked if I still wanted him to schedule a session. I said I had nothing to hide. He told me he would call me back so I could not use his name to find information about him on the internet. I hung up. Two of my intuitive friends told me not to schedule a session with him because of his negative energy. I made sure I asked Source if I was allowed to work with him, and I was given permission. He scheduled an appointment.

The night before the reading, his deceased mother came in. Her personality was so in my face!

She gave me their names and told me all about her son and his life. She really didn't let me get much sleep. On the day of the reading I opened the door when Jim arrived. I didn't see a car in the parking lot. Later he told me he had intentionally parked at another building so I wouldn't see his car. Not many people drove his type of car, and he thought his car would reveal his identity. He told me he was here to prove I was a fake, and he was going to record me. He said he was there to ruin my reputation. I still wasn't worried at all.

I said, "So Jim, I had a visit from your mom last night. Fran wouldn't leave me alone. She loves to talk. She told me all about you and how you need to change." Then I had his attention! He said there was no way that I could have known his name, or his mom's name.

Source talked through me and told Jim that if he didn't completely change his life, his cancer would come back. Jim jumped when Source told him about the cancer. He had just gotten a clean bill of health from his doctor after fighting cancer. His guides told him that it wasn't too late to make the changes, but he needed to do a 180 degree turnaround or the cancer would come back again. I explained about life's lessons and what Heaven was all about.

This meant Jim would have to completely change his life. Jim was a VP at a successful company who got his way by bullying and frightening employees. He thought the employees should fear him. I could tell he wasn't a boss that I could have ever worked for. He was such a dictator. Jim didn't even have a relationship with his sisters because he was so controlling and thought everyone was beneath him. He had an ego issue.

Jim left saying this was a lot for him to digest. He said he would listen to the reading again and think about what he would do. I could tell that he felt defeated. Since he was all about his ego, he didn't like what I told him.

Several weeks later I got an unblocked call from Jim, and he scheduled another session. We still stay in touch, and he calls for checkups. Jim thinks he has made the 180 degree change that was needed, but the angels show me things in his life that he is not doing with unconditional love. Jim eventually agreed that it is very hard to live with unconditional love. Jim was the one who threw a punch to solve fights. I'm happy to say that Jim is still cancer free and trying to grow God like.

When faced with a confrontation, someone living with unconditional love will not react in anger. We all take two steps forward and a half step back. That's how we learn. Don't beat yourself up about the half step back. Just learn why you took the half step back and look forward. We are all here to grow.

Hannah

My chiropractor called and asked if I could help one of his patient's get rid of a ghost in her house. I told him I would have to ask Divine for permission and would get back to him. I was told I could help. I had no idea how, but I always trust when I am told to proceed. When

I went to Hannah's duplex, she asked me what I felt.

I told her a man had hung himself in the bedroom closet. He didn't cross over to the light and now his spirit was earthbound. Hannah concurred. She told me several priests had visited her home but had been unable to help.

This earthbound moved things around in the house. She and her girls would find things missing all the time. Hannah's daughters had to sleep with her because of all of the negative energy that surrounded them. Their dog would always bark at nothing, but they knew something was there. They just couldn't see it. The presence of the earthbound created anxiety attacks for Hannah, and she was not able to work because of the attacks.

I didn't have any fear. I asked for God's light and protection to help Hannah and her family. Usually when I go to help someone with an earthbound, I talk the earthbound into crossing over into the continuous light that is always shining called Heaven. The earthbounds are usually angry. They think they are still alive and people can see them. It always takes some time to convince them to go to the light, but they usually cross.

The portal of Heaven was open. I started to talk to this earthbound, but there was no way he was going to listen to me. He had so much fear, guilt, and anger that he refused to even listen to me. Then it hit me. I needed to call in the archangels for help. As soon as I asked for their help, Michael, Raphael and Uriel arrived. One grabbed a shoulder, another archangel grabbed another shoulder, and the archangels took the earthbound to Heaven. The earthbound was facing me, kicking and screaming all the way to the light. Once the earthbound was in Heaven, he was calm and happy. This all happened in less than 10 minutes.

This was way too easy. Why wasn't I told to call the archangels for help the other times? But I already knew that answer: it just wasn't time. I stayed with Hannah for awhile to get to know her better. The next day, Hannah called. My first thought was that it had been too easy and it really hadn't worked. Hannah told me that their house was calm. There was no disturbance or negative energy around. We talked a few weeks later. The girls were sleeping in their own beds, and Hannah was back to work. It's been over six years, and Hannah has never had another incident from the earthbound.

Ben

Ben was a very successful executive at a large corporation. He was very analytical and business minded. He really didn't believe in my gifts. Ben's family did believe, and they were one of my biggest supporters. One day I had appointments with each of his children. Due to scheduling conflicts the venue was changed, and we ended up meeting in Ben's house. When I was getting ready to leave, Ben walked in. His wife asked him if he would like to sit down with me. I was taken back when he said yes. He came in with a pen and paper, and said he had no idea how this went. I explained the process.

His deceased parents came to visit. They talked about specific events in his life. Ben's dad even talked about Ben's schooling and the guns he owned. But Ben just took notes and was typically quiet. He agreed to what his parents showed me, but there wasn't any emotion shown. All he did was take notes and validate what his dad was showing me. His guides talked about how the butterfly was his sign and how to pay attention to butterflies.

Ben was an avid photographer, and he said he loved to shoot butterflies. Ben was also told about all the orbs he would see if he ever went back to see old pictures. I explained that orbs are spirit energies that want to show they are in the earth realm. Orbs are small circles that look like balls of light in a photo.

Then I was shown a vision of Ben on a bike ride where he hurt his hamstring. I described the scene and told him how to help his strained hamstring. Ben finally reacted! He was completely startled. He said there's no way I could have known anything about his hamstring injury because it just happened before he came in to talk to me. No one from his family even knew that it just happened. So I teased him and said, "Did you think I did all this research about your childhood and made it up about your parents being here?" He said that I could have asked his family enough questions to know enough about me to pull that off, but there was no way I could have made up the hamstring injury in his left leg.

I told Ben that I always want to be true, and I just need to be God's conduit. I won't make anything up. We had a very in depth spiritual conversation, and I opened his eyes to the truth on why we are here. Ben listened, took many notes, asked questions, and tried to process this like any analytical person would.

Several weeks later, Ben emailed me, and his family, the list of my predictions and how each one had come to fruition. He added that he received a confirmation message from his guides: on a recent bike ride, a butterfly hitchhiked on his leg and stayed with him for several miles.

It was so nice to watch Ben change and become that spiritual, loving person. I even noticed how it changed the dynamics of his family and how his family members grew spiritually. They all started mediating and opening their individual gifts. I always knew Ben had a family of very gifted, kindred souls. I was so blessed to have worked with such a beautiful family.

Barb

Barb, an acquaintance at work, told me that she had been going through money issues over and over. Each time, she felt like she was doing the right thing and learning from her lessons. She didn't understand why God kept giving her the same money issues over and over again. If God is unconditional love, then he wouldn't do this to her.

My guides told me that this wasn't a money issue. The lesson was about perseverance. When I shared what I heard, I saw a light bulb go on right above her head. She gave me a really big smile and said, "I get it now!" Just sharing those few words with her made her outlook so much brighter.

Sometimes we get way too caught up in the drama of life. Sometimes we need to step outside of the issue look at it again. Ask for help dealing with the speed bumps of life's lessons.

Cindy

Cindy told me she was planning to file for divorce. The paper work was finished, and the attorney was going to file the next day. Cindy wanted to know if her husband would commit suicide when he got the news because he had threatened to kill himself several times if she ever left him. I asked my guides to see her husband. All I saw was a very lonely man, and all I could say was that he was all alone. I did not see any actions to show me that he would harm himself.

Several weeks later I was told that when he received the divorce papers he quit his job immediately and went to be alone. A few days later, he committed suicide. Once I heard this I was so upset because I hadn't seen this ahead of time and couldn't help Cindy. I meditated and prayed upon this for many hours. I always say that I want to help and be a conduit from Source. I didn't think Source had allowed me to be a conduit to help Cindy.

Then a week later, I was finally told that suicide is never in anyone's contract. On Earth, we have free will. Free will can take over and nullify the contract so that a suicide can happen. I will never cast judgment on anyone because we are not allowed to judge others. We can only judge ourselves. My archangels told me that since suicide is never in someone's contract, that soul **must** return to Earth for another lifetime, and the next lifetime will be much harder. Remember that you are the only one who judges your life. You must trust me: once you are in the heavenly realms, you don't want to come back to Earth unless you want to move up the realms to be closer to Source. Earth has free will and ego, and these traits are not in the heavenly realm. Heaven is a true utopia.

Energy Exchange

I recently started to charge for my readings. I always thought the gifts were God given and since they were gifts, I shouldn't charge. I never wanted to jeopardize my gifts. One day in meditation I was told that I must exchange energy for readings, or it will hurt my energy. After I heard that, I had to test it because I wanted to make sure I heard it right. I usually can help people all day, and my energy is never affected. So I scheduled six sessions, one right after the other. At the end of the day, I got really sick and was completely exhausted for several days. So I need to always listen to what comes from Divine.

Isaiah Chapter 45, 5 - 7

I am the LORD, and there is no other, besides me there is no God; I equip you, though you do not know me that people may know, from the rising of the sun and from the west, that there is none besides me; I am the LORD, and there is no other. I create the light and make the darkness. I send good times and bad times. I, the LORD, am the one who does these things.

The passage explains that God created all; the light and the dark. We must each learn our lessons and grow to be God like.

I hope that with every breath you take, you will live by the Golden Rule, the only rule in Heaven: Treat people better than you ever wanted to be treated without fear, judgment and guilt. Even God doesn't judge. We judge ourselves when we cross over to Heaven. God is unconditional love. The more we live God like in every breath we take, the more we will elevate our souls up the realms of Heaven to be closer to God. The God I know and see does not have judgment, fear or guilt. The God I see in this body during meditation is unconditional, endless love. So if Heaven is forever, you will want to start being God like on Earth to elevate your soul in Heaven.

If we all are acting God like, we are not blaming anyone for our actions. We are taking responsibility for what we do. We understand everything on our life's path is for our personal growth and for the growth of our loved ones. When we are all acting God like, we can make Heaven on Earth.

May this life's journey be filled with life's lessons that help your soul grow. Please don't be the victim along your journey. Take ownership of your own growth. You can choose to stay in Heaven after visiting the viewing room and seeing where you have missed opportunities, but you can only reach the highest realm when you return to Earth and learn to live God like with every breath you take. I hope the lessons in this lifetime will elevate your soul in the heavenly realms so you will be closer to God's amazing energy. Your lessons are your blessings. Learn and grow from them while becoming God like.

Epilogue

When I was putting the final touches on this book, I received a powerful message during deep meditation. It felt like I was seeing a piece from another puzzle! The message told me that my close friends and I should start "the trueism movement." This would be a spiritual movement, not a religion. I was told that it should be called "trueism," with the word "true" completely spelled out; keeping the "e" in true.

My book, "What's the Meaning of Life...Life Lessons," explains what Heaven is about and that we come down to Earth to teach our souls to be God like. The trueism movement will teach people how to grow from their life lessons. The movement will raise our personal vibrational energies using music, gifted teachers, and so much more to help our souls remember the truth of why we are here on Earth.

I always say that I just see the truth in the heavenly realm and if people would understand the truth, life would be much simpler. I researched trueism and was unable to find a single reference for it. This was a sign that the message I had received was divinely driven, so I registered it as a trade mark and a website www.thetrueism.com.

We know everyone can't come to us in Canton, Ohio. We plan to travel to many countries to give people everywhere the opportunity to come to us, learn about trueism, and experience "trueism" resonating in their souls.

About the Author

Debbie Bryan

Debbie Bryan is a medium of multiple realms who works with archangels and angels to help guide others through life's journey. She is blessed with seeing, hearing, and knowing the angelic realm. Debbie was born with these gifts but never understood that everyone didn't see or hear the angels. Debbie believes it is her mission to contribute to a cause greater than herself. She does this by using her gifts as a connector with source in healings,

teachings, personal and group sessions. She is the messenger for angelic communication to groups and individuals. Debbie is also a healer by allowing the heavenly realm to direct the individual healing that is needed. She has been given a key to unlock the 12 strand DNA codes which is used in her healings and upgrades. Debbie also teaches a class called, Healing Your Life with the Angels.

Debbie's reading and healings include connecting with your deceased loved ones, talking to your angels, seeing the future, past and present. Debbie can facilitate Past Life Regressions, Emotional Release Therapy, Assisting Souls to Cross Over and Removing Attachments.

www.angeldebbie.com
www.yourspiritualhealer.com

Printed in the United States
By Bookmasters